T0381203

AuthorHouse™
1663 Liberty Drive
Bloomington, IN 47403
www.authorhouse.com
Phone: 1 (800) 839-8640

Published by AuthorHouse 09/03/2015

ISBN: 978-1-5049-2587-7 (sc)
978-1-5049-2588-4 (e)

Library of Congress Control Number: 2015912302

Print information available on the last page.

Any people depicted in stock imagery provided by Thinkstock are models,
and such images are being used for illustrative purposes only.
Certain stock imagery © Thinkstock.

This book is printed on acid-free paper.

authorHOUSE®

A Monkey Tale

Night of the Jungle Circus

Written and Illustrated by Ebony Skye

This book is dedicated to the friends that touch your life, and forever after, color it with the beauty of their love & laughter.

We love you, Chris & Sarah.

v

The moon lit up the starry night sky. It was past their bedtime, yet all the little monkeys were in a restless frenzy shuffling through the jungle trees.

"Please tell us the tale of the Crazy Critter Circus. Oooh! Please, Mr. Proboscis!" they begged.

"Oooh... Ooh, alright," said Mr. Proboscis as he made his way down through the branches. "Gather around little ones." And so he began to tell the tale of the night of the jungle circus...

Once upon a full midnight moon, many banana heaps ago, all of the Hairy Butt Witty Committee gathered around the old baobab tree...

"Order in the canopy!" shouted old Wilmer smacking his sugarcane. "It's time to take care of monkey business." All tails stood at attention. "Harvest moon is near. All you monkeys know what that means. It's time to -"

"Jungle Boogie!" interrupted Bozo as he skid up next to Wilmer for a booty bump!

"That's right!" said Wilmer. "This moon we'll throw the best jungle boogie ever! Time to put on our thinking caps."

Chacho looked around anxiously as all the other monkeys pulled out banana peels and plopped them on their heads.

"I fur-fur-g-g-got mine," said Chacho twiddling his tail. Biff smashed the last bit of banana in his mouth and handed the peel to Chacho "Gee, th-th-thanks Biff," said Chacho with a grin.

"No prob' ol' pal!" said Biff.

5

So, they all thought... And thought... And scratched...
And then, thought some more!

"That's it!" said Bozo breaking the silence. "I've got it!"
Everyone looked at Bozo. He was upside down tangled up in a
vine.

"What is it, Bozo?" asked Wilmer.

"I finally got that banana chunk out of my toe!" said Bozo.
"Mmmm... Delicious!"

Everyone grunted and then returned to thinking and
scratching.

7

Three howls and two hoots later, an unexpected visitor showed up. A purple-billed platypus wobbled up with a heavy chain clenched in his bill. A scorpion wearing a spiked collar tugged at the end.

"Well, hello Mr. Platypus," said Wilmer. "What brings you to this tail of the jungle?"

"Greetings Wilmer," said Mr. Platypus. "I was just taking Ed here for a stroll when I heard that you were holding a meeting with the Hairy Butt Witty Committee to plan this moon's jungle boogie." Ed jumped and snapped his pinchers. Mr. Platypus yanked back on his chain. "I have a business proposition for you."

Mr. Platypus went on to explain that he was the host of the Crazy Critter Circus.

"If you monkeys accept my offer," Mr. Platypus smirked, "my special guests will perform for the first time ever, their new act – The Abominable Stench."

The Hairy Butt Witty Committee thought it was strange to call it that.

"It will be a breathtaking, absolute knockout performance," said Mr. Platypus. "I assure you that!"

"I don't know..." said Felix. "I think he's pulling our tails." All the apes looked around skeptically and scratched their hairy heads.

And, well...

Mr. Mandrill Baboon just scratched his butt.

Mr. Platypus scanned the suspecting crowd with shifty eyes. He knew he had to sweeten the deal. "The deal includes a break-dancing camel," said Mr. Platypus matter-of-factly.

The monkeys looked at each other and grinned. "We'll take it!" everyone shouted at once. "It's a deal!" said Wilmer. All the monkeys jumped up and down and rattled the baobab branches. Everyone, except Felix that is...

Mr. Platypus just smiled.

Finally... The night arrived and the party was in full swing! All the jungle was in a frenzy! The gorillas beat their bongos. The orangutans clicked their claves.

All the other monkeys clapped their palms and smacked their hairy bellies to the jungle beat... or... Rustled playfully through the jungle vines... or...

21

Danced around, jumping, swinging and stomping their feet! All the monkeys had a great time!

They all agreed that it was, indeed, thee best jungle boogie ever! Even Señorita Sloth rated it a thumbs up.

BUTT...

WAIT!!!

There's more!...

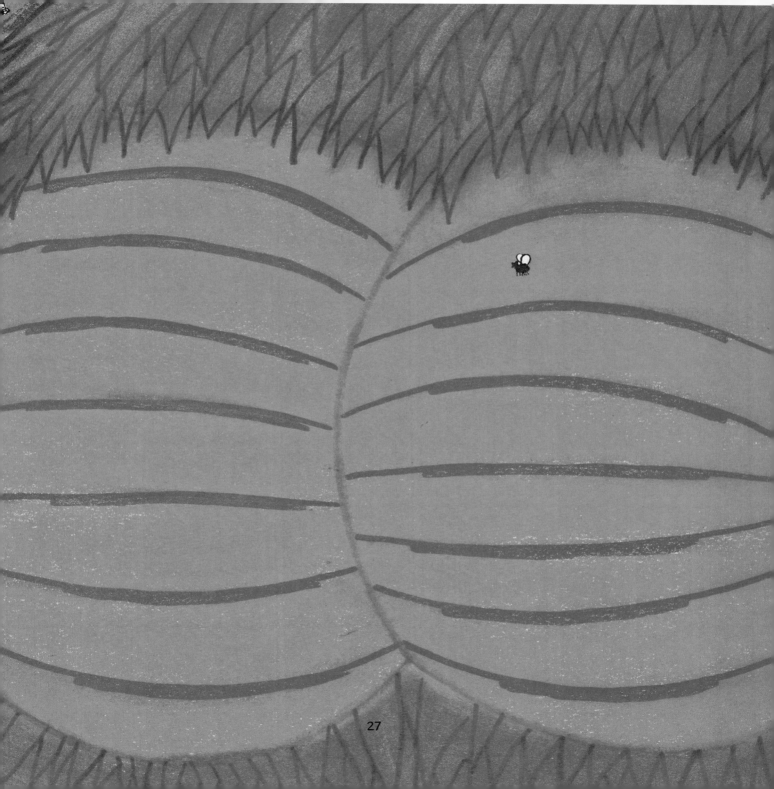

Even the vervet twins stopped picking the bugs off each other's backs to...

Watch the Crazy Critter Circus!

The Hard Rock'n Llamas threw a concert and danced in their pajamas! Then, the Gymnastic Giraffes flipped, flexed and flew fabulously through the air!

31

The Yodeling Purple Partly Polka Dotted Zebra was...

ASTRONOMICAL!

Next up, the Belly Flopping Walruses made a big splash! They were...

FLABBERGASTING!

The Hippos had a bean eating contest.

Hydro, the Break-Dancing Camel was...

TOTALLY AWESOME!!!

In fact, he was down right...

FANNNTASTIC!!!

The crowd went wild!

Then, Techno Sloth showed off his strobe light and tried to impress the crowd with his robotic grooves. But... Sloth was just too slow. Everyone threw mango pits and hooted him off the stage. Desperate for a quick save...

The Hip Hop'n Hippos had a dance off! It was a...

RIOT!

Then the stage announcer stepped out into the center of the rink. "And Last, but not Least!... The Crazy Critter Circus would like to present... The Premiere Performance of... Please Welcome!... Drum roll, Maestro!"

Da Doo Da Doo Da...
Dumm Dummm Doo...
Rat-a-tat-tat...
TAT!

"THE ABOMMMINABBBLE STENCH!!!"

Out stepped the Hippos to the center of the rink...

Along with a special guest veiled in purple riding poised on a donkey's back. Ned waited for his cue while all the jungle waited in silent anticipation. Then Mr. Platypus gave the signal!

Then, Ned unveiled the masked raider. There and behold was an exotic imported black and white striped creature doing a handstand!

It set off an evil smelling stench just as all the Hippos let their

BEANS BREEZE!!!

Suddenly, the earth began to...

RRRUMMMBBBLLLE!!!

The trees began to...

SSSHHHAKKKE!!!

Green Smog filled the jungle air. And there was a rancid, overpowering, absolutely breathtaking...

STENCH!!!

It was a real...

KNOCKOUT.

All because there really was...
An Abominable Stench.

"That night, all the jungle fell to sleep..." said Mr. Proboscis. "Even restless little monkeys like yourselves. Now little monkeys, the moral of this jungle tale is -"

"Ooh, ooh! I know!" said Joe-Joe. "Be wise. Lies come in disguise." Mr. Proboscis just stroked his chin.

"When you must scratch, there's always a catch?" said Cha-Cha with wide eyes. Mr. Proboscis just folded his hands and rested them across his belly. Joe-Joe and Cha-Cha looked at each other and scratched their heads.

Choo-Choo jumped to his feet. "I got it!" said Choo-Coo. "Don't trust strangers!"

Mr. Proboscis just chuckled. "No, no my silly little monkeys," said Mr. Proboscis with a grin. "The moral of this jungle tale is...

Never underestimate the power of a barrel of beans."

This book was created with love in honor of my best friend, Sarah. Her presence was always aglow with the richness of her love, laughter and beauty. Sarah's dimpled smile and joyful laughter forever fill the hearts of those whose lives she has touched.

Ebony Skye grew up a free-spirited country girl raised in the small village of Neosho, Wisconsin. Her love of nature, wildlife and far away places has always filled her imagination. Ebony's illustrations artfully share her eye for intense and brilliant colors. She is known for her playful nature, love of laughter and passion to inspire others.

Printed in the United States
By Bookmasters